Earlier Heaven

poems by

Elisabeth Farrell

Finishing Line Press
Georgetown, Kentucky

Earlier Heaven

With gratitude to my friends in writing and my teachers
With thanks and love to Charles, Maeve, and my mom

Copyright © 2018 by Elisabeth Farrell
ISBN 978-1-63534-614-5 First Edition
All rights reserved under International and Pan-American Copyright Conventions.
No part of this book may be reproduced in any manner whatsoever without written permission from the publisher, except in the case of brief quotations embodied in critical articles and reviews.

ACKNOWLEDGMENTS

Grateful acknowledgment is made to the editors of the publications in which these poems first appeared:
The Aroostook Review: "Veteran's Day at the Corner Store"
Color Wheel: "Meditation"
The Fourth River: "Mosquitoes"
Free Lunch: "Sweetser Street"
The Healing Muse: "Diagnosis"
Literary Mama: "April Storm"
Oak Bend Review: "Spring Rain"
North American Review: "Ronald Reagan"
Perigee: "Fragments from the Hospital"
The Sow's Ear Poetry Review: "Wild Blueberries"
Wild Apples: "Home"

Publisher: Leah Maines
Editor: Christen Kincaid
Cover Art: Charles Farrell
Author Photo: Nicole Derr
Cover Design: Elizabeth Maines McCleavy

Printed in the USA on acid-free paper.
Order online: www.finishinglinepress.com
       also available on amazon.com

Author inquiries and mail orders:
Finishing Line Press
P. O. Box 1626
Georgetown, Kentucky 40324
U. S. A.

Table of Contents

I

1	Home
2	Sweetser Street
3	Long Days Spent
4	Walls of Childhood
5	Wild Blueberries
6	Grandmother
7	To Be Amish
8	Mosquitos
9	Veteran's Day at the Corner Store
10	Ronald Reagan

II

13	Anniversary
14	Diagnosis
15	Psychiatrist's Office
16	April Storm
17	Fragments from the Hospital
18	Turtle
19	Spring Rain
20	Beets
21	Meditation
22	Bohemian Highway
23	Sea Rose
24	Sloth Orphan
25	Father
26	On the Shore
27	Box and Whisker

"A happy family is but an earlier heaven."

-George Bernard Shaw

ONE

HOME

This is the house of bones:
Clavicle, scapula, sternum,
the skeletons of mill workers before us,

and before them the place
where deer came to bed
every winter;

before the deer, the unimaginable
pines, thick and tall
as redwoods.

This is the house of femur, phalanges:
A woman so poor
she tied her hair with shoe laces.

It is not a sad house. It is one hundred
years strong, settled. It is our home now:
At night we watch the stars

from our bedroom skylight. They shine
like bones tossed into blackness
for a dog too lazy to fetch.

SWEETSER STREET

You can remember the chain link fence,
the abandoned field,
packs of boys riding ATVs,
doing wheelies like superheroes.

You can see the sewer hole,
the shack on a slab of concrete,
burned up bits of comic strips
sputtering from its chimney.

And you'll always be there, staring out of number six,
the two-story mint green New Englander,
looking out at the pigeons perched like dirty ornaments
on the branches of a single pear tree.

LONG DAYS SPENT

Roaming the neighborhood
we found a kitten stuck
in a baseball dugout;
we found a cemetery
deep in some forgotten woods.
We buried a hamster. We dug it up
a few weeks later, observed
the gel of its flesh,
the brilliant white bones.
We spied on a kindly old woman,
convinced she stuffed her bra.
We stuffed our own bras
with Kleenex; sometimes apples for a laugh.
We knew too much
about danger, knew too little
about ourselves. We trembled
together beneath the maples.
We sang to pass the time, conjured
spirits with séances and Ouija boards.
We hunted for ghosts, eager to see ourselves
through the eyes of the departed.

WALLS OF CHILDHOOD

Inside there are robins,
dozens gathered on the windowsill,
plucking worms out of the woodwork,
sticking their beaks into the window screen
as if they might escape.   But they will not,

neither they nor the turtles that huddle
in the dark corners, nor the snakes
entwined in their cold-blooded masses
beneath the bed, waiting for an innocent
to dangle its toes down like fishing lure.

Through the window the grass is brilliant green.
Mice chew eternally,
but even they cannot get free.
O the thick, unyielding walls
of a single dream, or one thousand…

WILD BLUEBERRIES

He brought them home in old coffee cans,
hundreds, thousands, some still holding on to stems.
Berries so small I wondered how they'd survived
being pinched between his fingers.

He offered them and I reached in,
hand like a cup, gently
shaking them into my palm.

He stared down at his hands
when I tried to call him Dad,
though I wanted to call him that,
even if it wasn't true.

Thank you, I tried to say,
for picking me wild blueberries.
One by one I ate them. Then, by the handful.

GRANDMOTHER

Master of needles
and yarn

like the bird
building her nest

you are serious

the way a mother of daughters
always is

in a world not made
for them

a shelter

sometimes you can do no more
than protect

yourself, a temple
of smoke and spirits

a song

you sing and bring news
no one wishes to hear

you sing like a crow
who does not sing at all

you are sunken

though somewhere
you soar

and I see you there
flashing your black wings

TO BE AMISH

We sang hymnals and *America the Beautiful*
all the way to Lancaster, my mother and I.
Nine-years-old and in the front of the bus,
I held the tour guide's microphone like a torch.
And when we got there, I believed
it was heavenly: carefully-tended
fields, horse and buggy, huge pies
and freshly-churned butter, women
and men in simple attire,
no zippers, no Velcro. Bonnets and aprons
and hay-filled mattresses. Homes
transformed into meeting places,
wooden benches lined up for God. Pure,
the way I thought life should be, devoted
to a higher calling, unlike the life I knew
in my little Maine town: the alcohol, the grief,
the father who could not be found. How I wanted
to be the girl walking a long dirt driveway,
dark braids falling neatly down her back,
lost in thought, eyes raised to the sky.

MOSQUITOES

He was immune to them, the mosquitoes that swarmed
around his head, around his bare hands holding the fishing pole.

He stood like a monument to steadiness,
unmoved by the buzz, the bites, the angry welts.

I peered through a head net,
swatted and slapped and stomped in mud.

I didn't care about the trout. My netted vision filtered out
the velvety cattails, the lily pads reflecting sun.

I could never be what I was not: his daughter.
I belonged only to my mother, father gone before I was born.

And he, standing silent at the edge of the pond—
he belonged to no one.

VETERAN'S DAY AT THE CORNER STORE

The boy is twelve
and nervous beneath
his camouflage jacket.

The crusty woman
smokes a cigarette
and fills in the details:

Doe. 20-gauge shotgun.
One hour ago.
First kill.

The boy gives her a dollar.
She gives him a registration tag
and a wink.

His eyes fall.
He tugs at his shirtsleeve
and uses it to wipe sweat

from his upper lip.
His hands are clammy
and suddenly old.

RONALD REAGAN

I liked you and your chimpanzee, your jellybeans, your astrology.
I sent you fan mail scrawled in third-grade cursive, loopy
and convinced: You are the greatest, Mr. President.
At night I curled up with my mother and watched
bombs drop on Libya. I packed my suitcase full of canned goods,
hid it under my bed, waiting for nuclear attack.
My mother adored you, even though you waged war
on women like her: poor, single mothers, humiliated
and humiliating. Would you believe the poor
have grown even poorer? Mercury must be stuck
in retrograde, stars misaligned, galaxies off course.
Don't be afraid to see what you see, you said,
but I am, of course. I am afraid of all that we see
and do not see clearly. Even you, Ronnie,
believed a tree's a tree, when I know it's actually
sunlight and water, clouds and thunder, ancestors
holding earth and sky together precariously.

TWO

ANNIVERSARY

There is a time I call Before.

I do not long for it,
but I will not forget it.

I remember the tiny turquoise
ring I buried for you,

ashes lifting over the tidal inlet,
a dusky heron looking on.

I remember the water
moving over the muddy flat,

returning to this place you loved.

DIAGNOSIS

After checking the stove over and over
to see what I'd seen and didn't believe—
burners off and cold—it occurred to me,

there must have been a portent in my past—

a forecast of this daily ritual, this circle
round and round the kitchen, flipping switches,
trying to contain a fire already raging.

PSYCHIATRIST'S OFFICE

Bromeliads line the window ledge,
their leaves a spiky border,
requiring so little
light and feeding, thriving
here at the edge of the sill,
their pink centers glossy,
the New England evening
deepening around them.

APRIL STORM

Flurry of snow, marvelous and blinding.
Through the window I watch it go down.
Thirty-foot pine limb on the ground,
the hundred-year-old apple tree broken
beneath its scented branches.

Men come to clean things up.
Chainsaws and hard hats and pick-up trucks.
Apple trunk, its center dark and hollow,
sliced into chunks, roots dug up
and fed through the chipper.

I watch, just minutes from learning
inside me there is no baby, only a sac:
black and empty on the ultrasound screen;
hours from laying my body flat on a steel bed,
legs spread, womb sucked clean.

FRAGMENTS FROM THE HOSPITAL

Behind the curtain
the old woman coughs, retches,
speaks into the intercom,
her voice high-pitched and ancient.
"Is that Hekate?" I ask a stranger staring down at me.

At night the IV drips
noiselessly into my vein.
I enter a funhouse where I am molested.
I crawl through a falling-down town,
shielding my head from the debris.

When I wake I am fed
applesauce from a baby food jar.
I hear the old woman behind the curtain
talking to her dog on the telephone:
"Good morning, Mama's girl."

Someone leads me to the shower room,
helps me disrobe. I am sewn up, bandaged.
Through the gauze I see
the lines of stitching, I see
I've survived again.

TURTLE

There it is, not much larger than a quarter, a turtle
in midday sunshine, at the center of the concrete sidewalk,
heading, so I think, to the pond across the street,
but stopped now in its trail by the dog's curious nose.
Head and feet pull in.
The dog's not interested, moves on.

My fingers are delicate, careful not to crush, desiring only to turn it over,
see its light belly, its tiny head and feet tucked in, a month after
my own egg opened into miscarriage.
Here is one that made it,
that will travel, if lucky, down the hill,
through the wild grasses and trillium that lead to the pond.

SPRING RAIN

Maple leaf like a hand

dangling limp, stripped

of last year's gold,

withered fingers and a palm

of indecipherable lines

on an otherwise bare tree.

BEETS

I never loved you
until now, torn yesterday
from the ground, a clump
of hearts buried—small, red,
(except one pale pink, almost
white), round—
and brought to light, shaken free

of soil. Who will do this
to me, I wonder. Who will pull me
out from under, clean me,
take me whole?
Will they love me or will
they learn to love me,
as I have you, slowly?

MEDITATION

Into my own heart
your voice is singing. It is long
and reaches out through

my eyes, softens
my face into a slow smile,
turns deeper and deeper until

finally my jaw drops
open, spacious as the sky,
the song becomes silence.

BOHEMIAN HIGHWAY

We were happy
and the days were long
and mild and everything
around us was new, old,
and new again. Every bend
brought changed light
and we chased it until
it changed again.
We thought ourselves
changed, believed
in the Road, wild
mustard flaming in fields,
thousands of cultivated vines.
We believed ourselves.
The words we said and didn't
say were perfect as the orange petals
of the California poppy—delicate,
but no less true.

SEA ROSE

Remember me, sea rose.
Remember me, your secret
love, the one
who leaned close,
whispered,
        Tell me
        what you know.

Fat hips of September,
ripe sea rose,
yellow centers damp with spray,
remember me, my fragrance
mixed with yours, blushing
cheeks and petals.

        Sea rose,
tell me nothing of love
is forbidden, is forgotten.

SLOTH ORPHAN

A stuffed bear will suffice
as makeshift mother. It's soft
and warm and seems almost
to hold you with its paws.
A stuffed bear will be fine

company throughout the long days
spent dozing in your cardboard box,
your wet nose dampening its faux
fur, your breath forming droplets of water
on its plastic snout.

You are grounded, tree hugger,
and life below the canopy is not gilt-
edged leaves and filtered mist.
Your curled claws have no use here,
your intolerance for stress will leave you

stricken. You're a lucky one,
little orphan. Someone has tried to save you
with their guilty conscience. Go on, love them
like your mother during the daylight,
but at night, climb as high as you can,
deep into the lungs of God.

FATHER

He barks like a carny
trying to hawk some cheap
stuffed animal. I keep shooting

until the fairground gates shut
and someone kindly leads me
out, empty-handed.

ON THE SHORE

The sadness
>of the whale
is enormous,

>and the crowd pouring
pails of water over it,
>helpless.

The whale,
>which already knows
its fate,

>has come ashore
to complete it amidst
>the onlookers who want the world

other than it is,
>who want resurrection
without death.

BOX AND WHISKER

> *"We see the world once, in childhood.*
> *The rest is memory."* –Louise Glück

Sometimes I see you
standing in your flannel shirt
thick with sweat at the chopping block
axe about to strike.
Your slicked back hair
shines in the moonlight.
The fragrance of pine
fills the air, beauty released
from your violence.

—

Once there was an injured robin.
You sheltered it in the grass,
under a laundry basket.
A bad idea in the first place.
It wasn't long before you found it
torn apart. Never mind
the damage you had done.
The robin—redemption—lost.

—

Everyday I opened the metal
door you built of scraps
from the shipyard.
Who did you think you were
to me, anyway? Everyday
I opened the door, hopeful
and afraid.

—

The night you died a dog
arrived at the door. Big, friendly
golden retriever. I hoped it was you,
transformed. In the morning,
it was gone. I wondered if
I'd ever known you.

—

Later we left that house
forever. There were others
I imagined were you, improved.
Never mind, I was wrong.
Isn't that always the trouble?

—

I'm not sure I ever really saw you.
Still, you existed. I know this
because of your absence.

—

And so it comes to mathematics,
a plotting of our sample
experience. There are outliers
to interrogate. There are other
samples to measure against.
It is work. It is difficult.

Note: Box and whisker plots are used to display quantitative sample population data, including minimum, median, maximum, quartile, and outlier points of data.

ELISABETH FARRELL lives with her husband and daughter in southern Maine. She received her Master of Fine Arts degree from Bennington College, where she was a Jane Kenyon scholar. Her poems have appeared in journals including *North American Review, The Fourth River, Literary Mama, The Sow's Ear Poetry Review*, and elsewhere. She also holds a Master of Public Administration and a Bachelor of Arts in anthropology, both from the University of New Hampshire. She is a project director at the University of New Hampshire Sustainability Institute, where she has worked for over 15 years.

www.ingramcontent.com/pod-product-compliance
Lightning Source LLC
LaVergne TN
LVHW041506070426
835507LV00012B/1364